FU[N]

Published in Great Britain in 1999
by Penny Publishing Limited.
www.pennypublishing.com

Written by Richard Breen.
Compilation copyright © 1999 Penny Publishing Limited.
Text copyright © 1999 Richard Breen.
Designer Tom Gordon.

All rights reserved. No part of this publication may be reproduced,
stored in a retrieval system, transmitted in any form or by any means,
electronic, mechanical, photocopying, recording or otherwise, without
the prior written permission of the copyright owner.

INTRODUCTION

Like everyone else, especially millionaires, you and I need more money. But let's try to remember the saying:

Money isn't everything: usually it isn't enough!

Richard Breen.

One only lends to the rich,
for good reason since the others
never pay you back.

Tristan Bernard (1866-1947),
French writer.

If you want to lose a troublesome visitor lend him money.

Benjamin Franklin (1706-1790),
American statesman.

When a fellow says it ain't the money but the principle of the thing, it's the money.

Frank Hubbard (1868-1930),
American humorist.

I like Gala more than my mother,
more than my father,
more than Picasso and even
more than money.

Salvador Dali (1904-1989), on his wife.

The meek shall inherit the earth but not the mineral rights.

John Paul Getty (1892-1976),
American businessman.

You are robbed on the Stock Market in the same way that you are killed in battle, by people you never see.

Alfred Capus (1857-1922),
French journalist and playwright.

There are people who have money and people who are rich.

Coco Chanel (1883-1971).

Half the money I spend on advertising is wasted, and the trouble is I don't know which half.

John Wanamaker (1838-1922),
American Retailer.

One must choose in life between making money and spending it. There isn't time to do both.

Edouard Bourdet (1887-1945),
French playwright.

What is most despicable about money is that it even brings talent.

Fedor Dostoievski (1821-1881),
Russian writer.

If you think nobody cares if you're alive, try missing a couple of car payments.

Earl Wilson (1907-),
American columnist.

There are three faithful friends -
an old wife, an old dog and
ready money.

Benjamin Franklin (1706-1790),
American statesman.

How can poverty be a vice?
Vice is rather pleasant.

Paul Leautaud (1872-1956),
French writer.

Sam Goldwyn, the American film producer, was haggling with George Bernard Shaw (1856-1950) over the cost of purchasing the film rights for Shaw's plays. Shaw finally refused to sell:

The trouble, Mr Goldwyn, is that you are interested only in art and I am interested only in money.

Whenever you receive a letter from a creditor write fifty lines upon some extra terrestrial subject, and you will be saved.

Charles Baudelaire (1821 67),
French poet.

Respectable means rich, and decent means poor. I should die if I heard my family called decent.

Thomas Peacock (1785-1866),
English novelist and poet.

It saves a lot of trouble if, instead of having to earn money and save it, you can just go and borrow it.

Winston Churchill (1874-1965).

By a continuing process of inflation governments can confiscate, secretly and unobserved, an important part of the wealth of their citizens.

John Maynard Keynes (1883-1946), quoting Lenin.

Jack Flyn, Reader's Digest,
on a lawyer's principle:

I believe a man is innocent until he runs out of money.

Poverty is no disgrace to a man, but it is confoundedly inconvenient.

Sydney Smith (1771-1845),
cleric and writer.

I've got all the money I'll ever need if I die by four o'clock.

Henry Youngman (1906-),
American comedian on inflation.

Creditors have better memories than debtors.

James Howell (1594-1666),
English writer.

Riches cover a multitude of woes.

Menander (c.342BC-c.290BC),
Greek dramatist.

In France, money is a great sin. That's why more and more Frenchmen go to confession in Switzerland.

Jacques Mailhot,
French humorist.

Let us not be too particular; it is better to have old second-hand diamonds than none at all.

Mark Twain (1835 1910),
American writer.

Money is the seed of money
and the first guinea is sometimes
more difficult to acquire than the
second million.

Jean Jacques Rousseau (1712-1778),
French philosopher.

I'd like to live like a poor man with lots of money.

Pablo Picasso (1881-1973).

Look at me. Worked myself up from nothing to a state of extreme poverty.

S.J. Perelman (1904-1979),
American humorist.

Success, for a man, is to have earned more money than his wife can spend.

Sacha Guitry (1885-1957),
French writer and actor.

It's better to give than to lend and it costs about the same.

Philips Gibbs (1877-1962),
English journalist.

My problem lies in reconciling my gross habits with my net income.

Errol Flynn (1909-1959),
American actor.

The man who won't loan money isn't going to have many friends - or need them.

Wilson Mizner (1876-1933),
American dramatist.

Money speaks sense in a language all nations understand.

Aphra Behn (1640-1689),
British writer.

Men only hate the miser because there is nothing to be gained from him.

Voltaire (1694-1778).

Nobody accepts advice
but everybody accepts money.
Money is therefore more valuable
than advice.

Jonathan Swift (1667-1745),
satirist and poet.

Money has no smell.

Vespasian,
Roman Emperor (AD69-79).

Of all the icy blasts that blow on love, a request for money is the most chilling and havoc-wreaking.

Gustave Flaubert (1821-1880), French writer.

No man's credit is as good
as his money.

E.W. Howe (1853-1937),
American journalist.

When a man needs money, he needs money, and not a headache tablet or a prayer.

William Feather.

If you aren't rich you should always look useful.

Louis Ferdinand Celine (1894-1961),
French writer.

When there is an income tax, the just man will pay more and the unjust less on the same amount of income.

Plato (c.428-347BC),
Greek philosopher.

When you don't have any money, the problem is food. When you have money, it's sex. When you have both it's health.

J.P. Dunleavy (1926-),
Irish writer.

Lenders have better memories than borrowers.

Benjamin Franklin (1706-1790),
American statesman.

It's a terribly hard job to spend a billion dollars and get your money's worth.

George Humphrey (1890-),
American economist.

What greater evil could you wish a miser than long life?

Publilius Syrus (1st century bc),
Roman writer.

You can only drink thirty or forty glasses of beer a day, no matter how rich you are.

Adolphus Busch (1856-1913),
American businessman.

Most of us hate to see a poor loser - or a rich winner.

Harold Coffin.

The want of money is the root of all evil.

Samuel Butler (1835-1902),
English author.

About tax: 'There was a time when a fool and his money were soon parted but now it happens to everybody.'

Adlai Stevenson (1900-1966), American Politician.

A fair price for oil is whatever you can get plus 10 per cent.

Ali Ahmed Altiga (1931-),
Saudi Arabian businessman.

Very often he that his money lends loses both his gold and his friends.

Charles Spurgeon (1834-1892),
English clergyman & writer.

Making money ain't nothing exciting to me.
You might be able to buy a little better booze than the wino on the corner. But you get sick just like the next cat and when you die you're just as graveyard dead as he is.

Louis Armstrong (1900-1971), American jazz singer.

He had so much money that he could afford to look poor.

Edgar Wallace (1875-1932),
British novelist.

Our charity begins at home and mostly ends where it begins.

Horace Smith (1779-1849),
English parodist.

No man should commend poverty but one who is poor.

St Bernard of Clairvaux (1091-1153).

I cried all the way to the bank.

Liberace (1973),
American entertainer.

He who tells a lie to save his credit wipes his nose on his sleeve to save his napkin.

James Howell (1594-1666),
English writer.

Napoleon had yet again caught his minister, Talleyrand (1754-1838), up to his treacherous dealings:

'Tell me, monsieur de Talleyrand, you have been receiving money from the Emperor of Russia? What were you selling him?'

'Nothing, sire', replied Talleyrand, 'I was buying his confidence.'

One must despise money,
especially small change.

Francois Cavanna,
French writer.

The last important human activity
not subject to taxation is sex.

Russell Baker (1925-),
American columnist.

If you pay peanuts,
you get monkeys.

James Goldsmith (1933-1997),
English businessman.

The loss of wealth is loss of dirt,
As sages in all times assert;
The happy man's without a shirt.

John Heywood (c.1497-c.1580),
British singer and epigrammist.

He that dies pays all debts.

William Shakespeare (1564-1616).

Money is like women.
You have to look after it in order
to keep it, otherwise it departs to
make somebody else happy.

Edouard Bourdet (1887-1945),
French playwright.

Nobody who has wealth to distribute ever omits himself.

Leon Trotsky (1879-1940).

The best way to help the poor
is not to become one of them.

Laringley Hancock (1909-),
Australian businessman.

If you want to know the value of money, try to borrow it.

Benjamin Franklin (1706-1790),
American statesman.

A fool and his money are soon parted. What I want to know is how they get together in the first place.

Cyril Fletcher.

The human species, according to the best theory I can form of it, is composed of two distinct races, the men who borrow and the men who lend.

Charles Lamb (1775-1834),
British essayist and humorist.

Let us be happy and live within our means, even if we have to borrow money to do it.

Artemus Ward (1834-1867),
American humorist.

The best way to make everyone poor is to insist on equality of wealth.

Napoleon Bonaparte (1769-1821).

What I call loaded I'm not. What other people call loaded I am.

Zsa Zsa Gabor (1921-),
Hungarian born American actress.

Young people, nowadays, imagine that money is everything, and when they grow older they know it.

Oscar Wilde (1854-1900).

If you would know what the Lord God thinks of money, you have only to look at those to whom he gives it.

Maurice Baring (1874-1945),
British poet & writer.

Money can't buy friends; but you can get a better class of enemy.

Spike Milligan (1918-),
British comedian.

A rich man is nothing but a poor man with money.

W.C. Fields (1880-1946),
American comedian.

Frugality when all is spent
comes too late.

Seneca (4bc-65ad),
Roman philosopher & playwright.

There are few ways in which a man can be more innocently employed than in getting money.

Samuel Johnson (1709-1784),
British writer and lexicographer.

A bank is a place that will lend you money if you can prove that you don't need it.

Bob Hope (1903-),
American comedian.

It doesn't matter if you're rich or poor, as long as you've got money.

Joe Louis (1914-1981),
American boxer.

The Income Tax has made more liars out of the American people than golf has.

Will Rogers (1879-1935),
American Humorist.

It is better to have a permanent income than to be fascinating.

Oscar Wilde (1854-1900).

The safest way to double your money is to fold it over once and put it in your pocket.

Kim Hubbard (1868-1930),
American humorist.

As a general rule, nobody has money who ought to have it.

Benjamin Disraeli (1804-1881),
British Prime Minister.

The only thing I like about rich people is their money.

Lady Astor (1879-1964),
American born British politician.

Just be glad you're not getting all the government you're paying for.

Will Rogers (1879-1935),
American humorist in 1929.

I haven't heard of anybody who wants to stop living on account of the cost.

Kim Hubbard (1868-1930),
American humorist.

The only thing that hurts more than paying an income tax is not having to pay an income tax.

Lord Thomas Duwar.

Misers are very good people;
they amass wealth for those who
wish their death.

Stanislaus Leszcynski (1677-1766),
Polish King.

Everyone, even the richest and most munificent of men, pays much by cheque more lightheartedly than he pays in specie.

Max Beerbohm (1872-1956),
British writer.

> Think about all those people in automobiles, driving about with their debts.
>
> Elizabeth Hardwick (1916-).
> American writer.

If you can count your money, you don't have a billion dollars.

J. Paul Getty (1892-1976),
American businessman.

I'm tired of love: I'm still more tired of Rhyme.
But money gives me pleasure all the time.

Hilaire Belloc (1870-1953),
British writer.

Many speak the truth when they say that they despise riches, but they mean the riches possessed by other men.

Charles Caleb Colton (1780-1832),
British clergyman.

Money doesn't always bring happiness. People with ten million dollars are no happier than people with nine million dollars.

Hobart Brown,
American writer.

When it is a question of money,
everybody is of the same religion.

Voltaire (1694-1778).

Very few people can afford
to be poor.

George Bernard Shaw (1856-1950),
British playwright.

Early to bed, early to rise, work like hell and advertise.

Dr Scholl of Scholl shoes,
American tycoon.

Charity - What am I supposed to do with the money I earn? Give it back?

Rod Stewart (1945-),
Rock singer.

No rich man is ugly.

Zsa Zsa Gabor (1921-),
Hungarian born American actress.